Everyday Type

An introduction to using type on your computer

Richard Hunt

Everyday Type

ISBN **978-0-9561604-2-3**

Published by

Richard Hunt
23 Garnet Lane
Tadcaster
North Yorkshire
LS24 9LD

Produced using Serif PagePlus X7 running on Microsoft Windows 8.1 Pro.

All product names and trademarks acknowledged.

Contents

Points and picas....................37

Paragraph Alignment 38

Hyphenation...........................41

Introduction

Communicating your message, and doing so effectively, has never been so important as it is today.

Desktop computers and laser printers offer a wealth of creative possibilities unthinkable just a few years ago when the most sophisticated option that non-specialists had access to was a typewriter.

Using desktop publishing (DTP) software it is relatively straightforward to create page layouts and advertisements for distribution as printed items, as PDF files or even as e-books.

Although the means to produce stunning finished items is now so widely available, many people don't use it fully.

Learning a little bit about the underlying principles of type and design can help you to achieve better results, and this little book shows some of the basics.

Richard Hunt,
Tadcaster, January 2014.

Typography and DTP

What is typography?

Typography (from the Greek words *typos* (form) and *graphy* (writing) is the name for the technique not just of arranging type on the page but also for type design, and modification, altering the outlines and glyphs which represent type digitally.

For many people it means nothing beyond choosing a typeface and a size, but ignoring other aspects. Alignment, line length, leading (line spacing), tracking (the spaces between groups of letters) and kerning (the space between pairs of letters) are really quite basic.

In contemporary use, the practice and study of typography is very broad, covering all aspects of design and application. This includes typesetting and type design, handwriting and calligraphy, lettering on posters, signs and advertising plus measuring its effectiveness, readability and legibility.

What is DTP?

DTP stands for desktop publishing. Broadly, it's the process of arranging graphical and text elements together on a page using a computer, so that it is ready for output.

The term is mostly applied to creating page layouts with software like Adobe InDesign and QuarkXpress, Serif PagePlus or Microsoft Publisher. Word processing programs like Microsoft Word, OpenOffice Writer and so on can be used for basic desktop publishing purposes.

Full desktop publishing combines typesetting (choosing fonts and the text layout), graphic design, page layout (how it all fits on the page), and printing the document. Word processing software doesn't give the same amount of control.

The line dividing word processing, DTP and page layout in general has become less and less distinct since the use of computers became routine.

Typeface or font?

Particularly in word-processing, desktop publishing and web design, these terms tend to be used to mean the same thing, but strictly speaking *they're not*.

In traditional typography using metal type, a **typeface** refers to a set of characters which have the same general appearance, for example Palatino. Typefaces often, but not always, have **bold**, *italic* and ***bold-italic*** variants (usually known as weights).

In movable type typesetting, the term *font* refers to a specific size and weight of a typeface, because each typeface and size combination requires a different set of metal type. However, in digital typography, each character is represented by a glyph which is a mathematical description of its outline. Computer software converts the outline into tiny dots for screen display or printing.

The right type

Selecting a typeface to use for your publication is vitally important as your choice affects the publication's **legibility** and **credibility**.

With literally thousands of digital fonts available to choose from, how can you make the right choice?

Whether you are designing a small leaflet or a broadsheet newspaper, you need to take great care when you are choosing the typefaces which you are going to use.

To a large extent, the typefaces which you select will be determined by the kind of image which you want to project and what sort of content you want to get across.

It's very important that you use a typeface which meets your target readership's expectations. Some faces are instantly serious. Others **just aren't**.

Before you start work

Before specifying your own design, it's a good idea to take a look at what your competitors are doing (even something like a parish church newsletter has to compete for attention with other printed items).

- Which typefaces are other similar publications using, or just as importantly, *not* using?
- Are they using hyphenation?
- Are they using justification?

Other factors need to be considered as well.

- What sort of layout do they have?
- Do your rivals have photographs or use clipart and illustrations to make their point more clearly?
- Are they making use of colour, and if so, to what extent?

Not least, you need to think about how your final copies will be produced. It's no good using a typeface with fine detail on a beat-up inkjet loaded with the cheapest copier paper as the ink may bleed into the fibres, smudge and make the type unreadable.

In 1967 the British Standards Institution published a Standard on the *Classification of Typefaces* (BS29612:1967) which contains fairly precise definitions for the various categories and even though it's nearly fifty years old, it's still a pretty good starting point. Over the next few pages, we'll take a quick look at each of the main categories.

Serif typefaces

Serif typefaces have small bars at the ends of their strokes. They're probably the most frequently used typefaces for books, newspapers and magazines.

Modern serif typefaces

Modern serif typefaces first became available in the latter part of the eighteenth century. The first series of 'modern' serif typefaces were originally designed by the renowned Italian printer and typographer Giambattista Bodoni in 1798.

Their main feature is a very strong contrast between the thick and thin lines in the letter forms. The vertical lines are very heavy with thin horizontals, long and fine serifs.

In fact, because the horizontals and the serifs are so fine, modern serif fonts can be less readable than transitional or old style serif typefaces.

Many currently available modern serif typefaces include Bodoni in their name.

Bodoni BT

Initially rough, but then waxy
Initially rough, but then waxy
Initially rough, but then waxy
Initially rough, but then waxy
1234567890 *1234567890*
"£$%^&*@#?"
"£$%^&*@#?"

Bodoni è un tipo di carattere con grazie disegnato da Giovanni Battista Bodoni (1740-1813), caratterizzato da un alto contrasto tra le linee spesse e quelle sottili. È il classico esempio di font con grazie moderno.

Old style serif typefaces

Old style typefaces originated in the earliest days of movable type during the late fifteenth century. The thinnest parts of letters are at an angle to the stem rather than at the top and bottom. The contrast between thick and thin lines is generally subtle and old style serif fonts are rated highly for readability.

Old style designs are further divided into *Humanist* or *Venetian* such as Bitstream's Venetian 301, Berkeley Old Style and Centaur and *Aldine* or *Garalde* typefaces like Bitstream's Aldine 401, Garamond, Goudy Old Style and Palatino

Palatino became extremely widespread and popular, possibly to the point of being overused, in the mid-1980s when it was selected as one of the built-in typefaces for the Apple LaserWriter desktop laser printer (Times, Helvetica, Avant Garde, Century Schoolbook and Zapf Chancery were the others).

The Linotype version of Palatino is included with Windows 8.

Garamond, usually the Adobe version, is one of the most widely used typefaces for book publishing.

GaramondNo8

Initially rough, but then waxy

Initially rough, but then waxy

Initially rough, but then waxy

Initially rough, but then waxy

1234567890 *1234567890*

"£$%^&*@#?" *"£$%^&*@#?"*

« Garamond » est le nom donné à un groupe de polices serif, d'après le graveur Claude Garamont, à l'origine de la famille des « garaldes ». La plupart des polices d'écriture qui portent aujourd'hui le nom de « Garamond » sont dérivées du travail ultérieur

Transitional serif typefaces

Transitional serif typefaces (which fall between modern and old style, hence their name) emerged during the middle of the eighteenth century. The differences between thick and thin lines are more obvious than in an old style typeface, but not so much as in modern serif fonts.

They are what most people will recognise as a serif typeface as this category includes the classic designs of Times New Roman (1932) and Baskerville (1757).

Other transitional serifs include Bookman, Caslon, Century, Georgia, Plantin, and Utopia.

It's important to remember that classification as *Old Style,* *Transitional* or *Modern* is **not** always an indication of when a particular typeface was originally designed. John Baskerville's eponymous typeface, classified as transitional, appeared in 1757, but Georgia which is also a transitional face did not appear until 1993.

Times New Roman

Initially rough, but then waxy
Initially rough, but then waxy
Initially rough, but then waxy
Initially rough, but then waxy
1234567890 *1234567890*
"£$%^&*@#?" *"£$%^&*@#?"*

Times New Roman is a serif typeface designed by Victor Lardent and Stanley Morison for The Times. It made its debut in the 3 October 1932 issue of The Times newspaper and the design was released for commercial sale in 1933

Typography   modern Bodoni BT

Typography old-style Palatino

Typography transitional Plantin

Slab serif typefaces

Slab serif—also called Egyptian—typefaces, which first appeared about 1800, do not have much contrast between their thick and thin lines. The serifs are often the same thickness as the vertical. Because of this, slab serif fonts have a bold, rectangular appearance which makes them very good for use on signs and posters communicating a no-nonsense message.

In Britain, the Great Western Railway used a slab serif letter style for its cast brass locomotive name and number plates.

Examples of slab serif typefaces include Clarendon, Rockwell and Courier.

ClarendonBlk BT

Initially rough, but then
1234567890
"£$%^&*@#?"
"£$%^&*@#?"

Route 285 operates to Hatton Cross and Heathrow Central Bus Station for Terminals 1, 2 and 3. Buses operate every 10 minutes during the day, 15 minutes in the evenings and on Sundays and 30 minutes throughout the night.

Sans-Serif typefaces

Sans-serif typefaces are often used for display typography such as signs, headlines, and when visual clarity rather than high readability is needed. On web pages they're often used because serifs can be difficult to read on-screen. Sans-serif typefaces are also known as *lineale*.

Sans-serif designs first began to appear and be used at the turn of the eighteenth and nineteenth centuries. Before "sans-serif" became the usual term, "gothic" was a common description for this sort of design; it lingers on in font names like Franklin Gothic.

Grotesque sans-serif typefaces

Grotesque sans-serif typefaces are early sans-serif designs, such as Grotesque, Akzidenz Grotesk, and Franklin Gothic.

The term dates back to 1832 when William Thorowgood used it to describe the sans-serif type including lowercase letters produced by his Fann Street Foundry in London

"Grotesque" came from *grotesco*, 'of the cave' in Italian, and not because the design was thought ugly. The variant *Grotesk* is a Germanicised version of the term.

Franklin Gothic Medium

Initially rough, but then waxy

Initially rough, but then waxy

Initially rough, but then waxy

Initially rough, but then waxy

1234567890 *1234567890*

"£$%^&*@#?" *"£$%^&*@#?"*

Such are some of the minor experiences which, though not very sensational in themselves, are yet part of the every-day work of an "intelligence agent" (alias a spy)..

Neo-grotesque sans-serif typefaces

Neo-grotesque (also known as *Transitional* or *Realist*) sans-serif typefaces are the most common sans-serif fonts. Relatively straight in appearance with less line width variation than Humanist sans-serif typefaces, neo-grotesque designs are quite plain and anonymous.

This group of typefaces can be regarded as the "boringly-dull-but-safe" choice.

Arial

Initially rough, but then waxy

Initially rough, but then waxy

Initially rough, but then waxy

Initially rough, but then waxy

1234567890 *1234567890*

"£$%^&*@#?" *"£$%^&*@#?"*

Such are some of the minor experiences which, though not very sensational in themselves, are yet part of the every-day work of an "intelligence agent" (alias a spy).

Well-known examples include Bell Centennial (designed for AT&T in 1976, specifically to stay legible at small sizes), Helvetica, Univers, and Arial.

Humanist sans-serif typefaces

Humanist fonts are more calligraphic than other sans-serif typefaces, with some variation in line width and more legibility than other sans-serif fonts.

Examples of fonts designed in the print era include Johnston, Gill Sans, Myriad, Frutiger and Optima.

Examples designed in the computer era

Humanist 521 BT

Initially rough, but then waxy

Initially rough, but then waxy

Initially rough, but then waxy

Initially rough, but then waxy

1234567890 *1234567890*

"£$%^&*@#?" *"£$%^&*@#?"*

Such are some of the minor experiences which, though not very sensational in themselves, are yet part of the every-day work of an "intelligence agent".

include Calibri, Segoe UI, Trebuchet MS, Tahoma and Verdana (all of these designs are included with Windows 8).

Geometric sans-serif typefaces

Geometric sans-serif typefaces have a design based on geometric shapes. Usually the letter 'O' will look circular and lower-case letters like 'a' and 'e' will be based on a partial circle and straight lines. Geometric sans-serif fonts look and feel very modern. For example, Futura and its lookalikes are often associated with the Bauhaus architectural style.

Geometric sans-serif fonts tend to be used mostly for headlines and captions rather than for body text.

Futura BK BT

Initially rough, but then waxy
Initially rough, but then waxy
Initially rough, but then waxy
Initially rough, but then waxy
1234567890 *1234567890*
"£$%^&*@#?"
"£$%^&@#?"*

Such are some of the minor experiences which, though not very sensational in themselves, are yet part of the every-day work of an "intelligence agent".

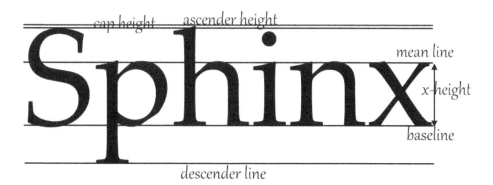

Script typefaces

Script typefaces simulate handwriting, either cursive (joined-up) or calligraphic (confusingly also known as italic). Simulate, because of course type can never reproduce the slight irregularities of real handwriting.

Script designs do not usually have bold or italic variants and tend to be used to give an informal or relaxed look. Most people find text set in script typefaces more difficult to read quickly than text set in serif or sans-serif typefaces. This means that they're normally used for short texts like logos or invitations and menus.

Cursive script typefaces

Cursive script typefaces can be further divided into casual and formal.

Casual script typefaces include Brush Script, Segoe Script, Mistral, Kaufmann and Bitstream's Stacatto series.

The Castle makes the perfect setting for any corporate event whether it be a meeting or dinner. SEGOE SCRIPT

A typical use for a casual script typeface is as a "friendly" introductory text on a brochure.

The setting is stunning, the service is friendly and efficient, and the catering is exceptional.

FREEHAND575 BT

It's important to note that script fonts often need to be set at a much larger size than text set in a 'normal' face so that they remain readable, as genuine handwriting is usually fairly large.ALT

16

Formal script designs resemble the flowing copperplate handwriting as used in the eighteenth and nineteenth centuries, for example Ancestry SF, Embassy BT or English157 BT.

The setting is stunning, the service is friendly and efficient, and the catering is exceptional.

COMMERCIALSCRIPT BT

Calligraphic typefaces

Calligraphic designs are not joined up. Each letter is quite distinct.

The setting is stunning, the service is friendly and efficient, and the catering is exceptional.

ZAPF CHANCERY

Perhaps the best-known calligraphic design is Zapf Chancery in its medium italic version which was very popular, almost to the point of becoming over-used, during the 1990s.

Hand print typefaces

The final category in this group resemble hand-written printing, and include designs like Comic Sans and Dom Casual.

A well regulated militia being necessary to the security of a free state, the right of the people to keep and bear arms shall not be infringed. COMIC SANS

Mostly, they're not very attractive. Comic Sans in particular screams '*Amateur At Work*'. Dom Casual dates back to 1951 and so it is hardly surprising that it looks a bit retro.

Blackletter typefaces

Blackletter typefaces, first used when the process for moveable-type printing with metal type was invented in the mid-15th century, resemble the blackletter calligraphy then in use.

They had been largely replaced for use in body text by serif typefaces—those known today as *'old-style'*— by the mid-16th century, at least in Britain, France and Italy.

Because it is so hard to read quickly, especially if you aren't used to it, in modern use blackletter type is found only for things like letterheads and ornamental items.

In Germany and Austria on the other hand, the variant known as *Fraktur* (which means 'broken'), continued in general use for books, newspapers and official printing until 1941 when it was denounced by the Nazis as being 'Jewish'.

Pfeffer Medieval

Initially rough, but then waxy

1234567890

"£$%^&*@#?"

Such are some of the minor experiences which, though not very sensational in themselves, are yet part of the every-day work of an "intelligence agent".

Pfeffer Simpelgotisch

fränkischer Straßenbahn Gesellschaft

1234567890

"£$%^&*@#?"

"£$%^&*@#?"

Als Gregor Samsa eines Morgens aus unruhigen Traumen erwachte fand er sich in seinem Bett zu einem ungeheuren Ungeziefer verwandelt.

After the German surrender in 1945 its use was of course allowed again but it is nowadays only used for things like shop fronts, newspaper mastheads and trademarks.

Fraktur has become, in effect, a decorative font.

Some versions use the "long-s" (ſ) instead of a normal 's'.

Most blackletter type does not have proper italic or bold variants because it is already very heavy.

Fette Deutsche Schrift
Fränkischer Straßenbahn-
Gesellschaft
1234567890
"£$%^&*@#?" "£$%^&*@#?"

Als Gregor Samsa eines
Morgens aus unruhigen
Traumen erwachte fand er sich in
seinem Bett zu einem ungeheuren
Ungeziefer verwandelt.

Some software will let you use a 'synthesised' bold or italic but they are a clumsy workaround and best not used. They look awful, and *will* cause output errors especially when making a PDF file.

Monospaced typefaces

Monospaced (fixed-width) typefaces use the same width for every character. In variable-width fonts some characters (like w and m) are wider than others and some (like i) are narrower. They resemble typewriter output and are mostly used for computer programming, E-Mails and laying out tabulated data.

Courier New, originally drawn for the IBM *Selectric* typewriter range, is perhaps the best-known monospaced font.

Consolas
Initially rough, but then
Initially rough, but then
Initially rough, but then
Initially rough, but then
1234567890 *1234567890*
"£$%^&*@#?" "£$%^&*@#?"

Such are some of the
minor experiences which,
though not very
sensational in
themselves, are yet part
of the every-day work of
an "intelligence

Display typefaces

Display typefaces are designed for decorative and advertising purposes, often at large sizes, and are not suitable for body text.

For example, a word or two set in Decorated 035 might be okay:

DALEK

But anything more QUICKLY BECOMES HARD TO READ, especially at smaller sizes or when mixed with 'normal' text.

Very often, display typefaces do not even have lowercase letters. And things like currency symbols are often missing too.

Symbol and Dingbat typefaces

Symbol (also known as *Dingbat* or *Pi*) typefaces are made up of things such as decorative bullets, clock faces and timetable icons rather than normal text characters.

Wingdings is a dingbat font included with Microsoft Windows.

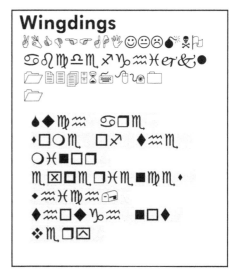

Which typeface is best?

This is a bit of an 'it depends...' question. I've never yet seen a newspaper which does not use a serif typeface for its articles.

In newspapers, and a lot of publications, one very commonly used serif typeface (probably the most widely used in fact) is Times New Roman. One of the main advantages of Times New Roman is that it is so familiar to just about every reader (it has been included with every copy of Windows sold since Windows 3.1) that it is a background item, read almost un-noticed and allowing the reader to concentrate on the story.

That's very important. Anything too radical and different puts people off. You need to consider what you readers are used to, and what they expect to see. Equally, it's very important not to look identical to your competitors or your publication will not get the attention you want it to.

Times New Roman's near-universal presence is a plus from the production point of view as well. 'Everyone' has it on their computer, which is handy if several people need to work on the same item on different PCs.

Some fonts are perhaps over-used: Helvetica and Arial spring to mind. Even the elegant Gill Sans family is used by both the BBC and the Post Office. Gill Sans was also used by the pre-1948 LNER, the nationalised British Railways until 1966 and the National Bus Company into the mid-1970s.

If you look carefully at most publications—printed or web— you will notice that they stick to basically a couple of typefaces, using bold for headlines and possibly italics for things like captions.

Another frequently-used tactic in magazines and catalogues is to use a sans serif font for headings and subheads but a serif face for body text.

One of the worst things which inexperienced desktop publishers do is to let their software install all of the optional fonts and then proceed to use as many of them as possible on each page.

It's just not necessary and you end up with a messy document that's hard to read.

In designs with few words, the rules about when to use different typeface styles are indistinct. A sans-serif, script or blackletter typeface might very well 'work' as part of a logo or on a sign.

Whether or not the description of 'typeface' or 'font' is entirely appropriate for the text in items which are not printed in the conventional ink-on-paper sense is another matter.

I'd say that in the contemporary era it is appropriate as virtually all design work is now done on desktop computer software and output via some kind of digital device.

What's in a name?

Something else which is ready and waiting to trap the unwary is that typefaces with similar, or even identical, names from different vendors can be different enough in design to not match properly.

This can be a problem if you are sharing documents with other users or sending work out to be printed by a commercial printer,who might not have exactly the same fonts available.

Some fonts have "lookalikes" with different names but which are very similar visually, for example the Bitstream Dutch 801 family or URW's NimbusRomanNo9 are so close to Times New Roman that the differences are hardly noticeable to the normal reader. Even so, it's not a good idea to put them next to each other.

The quick red fox   TIMES NEW ROMAN

The quick red fox   DUTCH801 ROM BT

The quick red fox   NIMBUS ROMAN NO9

Back in the early 1990s, fonts were very expensive to buy on their own, and it became normal practice, particularly at the consumer end of the market, for software companies to bundle fonts with their DTP and drawing programs.

The idea was supposedly to give the user more choice and to add perceived value to the products. However, it soon became a bit of a farce as marketing departments rushed to splash ever greater numbers of **FONTS INCLUDED** on their packaging so that they would appear to be giving better value for money than their competitors.

Frankly, this isn't very helpful. Some bundled fonts are not that good, and on a Windows machine you soon end up with a long and confusing fonts menu.

Lookalike fonts can be very good indeed but others are, to put it mildly, not very good and some are just rip-offs. A font from a "Thousand typefaces for a fiver" CD is extremely unlikely to be as good as "the genuine article" from the original publisher.

Of course, that does not mean that every free or low-cost font is rubbish. Some are produced by dedicated hobbyists, and some are definitely commercial. For example, Microsoft Office and Windows itself include several excellent fonts which have been carefully designed to look good both on screen and in print. Most desktop publishing and design software includes a selection of fonts, although just how useful some bundled fonts are is debatable.

Giving away lots of fonts with software has also given rise to the perception that fonts are a cheap commodity, which is definitely not the case for well-designed items. This has to a certain degree devalued the whole design process.

The letters BT or BTN after a typeface name indicate a Bitstream version, and although the names might be confusing and not bear much relation to the original[1], the typefaces are excellent.

---

[1] Usually due to the copyright status of the original design's name. For example, Humanist521 BT/Gill Sans, Zapf Calligraphic BT/Palatino, Swiss821 BT/Helvetica.

Exclusivity

A few newspapers and some other organisations have commissioned their own, exclusive, digital typefaces.

In the UK, two examples are *The Guardian* (and its Sunday sister, *The Observer*) and *The Daily Telegraph* and *The Sunday Telegraph*. This is of course vastly expensive and out of the question unless you are a really major company. *Deutsche Bahn AG*, the German railway network, has a set of exclusive font designs which are used for everything from timetables to station signs and train liveries as part of their corporate identity standard.

Sometimes the designs eventually become available commercially at the expensive end of the market (you can buy the *Economist 101* font family used by *The Economist*, but it will cost nearly £120).

For many years the Volkswagen group made use of the Futura family, but this was replaced by the specially designed VAG Rounded, in use between 1978 and 1992.

Others remain extremely tightly controlled. The distinctive typeface used by Transport for London (TfL), *New Johnston*, is only available for internal use and to TfL contractors. The *original* Johnston design which dates from 1916 has been released in a commercial deal with the TfL Museum by the P22 foundry as *P22Underground*.

Another example of a tightly-controlled design is the *GE Inspira* family which was designed by Michael Abbink around 2002 as part of the US General Electric Company's corporate identity, projecting a *"Clear, Precise, and Modern"* image. It has four styles, GE Inspira Book, GE Inspira Regular, GE Inspira Pitch (a bit bolder, for use on-screen), and GE Inspira Small Caps.

GE Inspira is only supposed to be available to General Electric employees or contractors, but unauthorised copies can easily be found on the internet.

In the mid-1960s the British Rail Design Panel endorsed the Rail Alphabet font which was used as part of the blue-and-grey 'Modern Image' introduced with the end of steam traction.

British Rail itself has long since gone, but Rail Alphabet is *legally required* for some safety and operational purposes.

It was also used by the NHS, especially on signs, but has now been replaced by Frutiger.

- In most situations, Bitstream's **Humanist 777** is an acceptable substitute for Frutiger.

A revised and digitised version of Rail Alphabet is available commercially; it's used throughout the British government's gov.uk website as shown below.

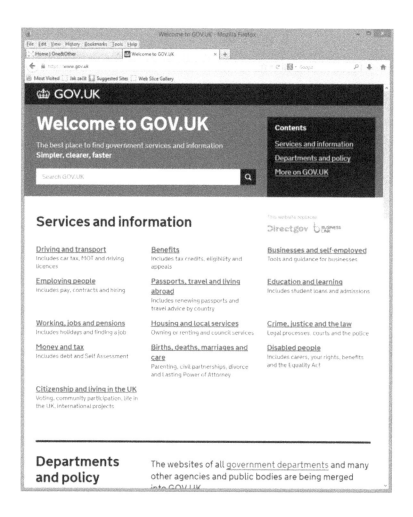

Windows system fonts

Microsoft include a fair number of typefaces with Windows.

They are skewed towards on-screen rather than print use, but do include enough choice for most everyday documents.

As well as the fonts listed in this section there are fonts for non-western scripts, for example Shonar Bangla used by the Bengali alphabet (Bengali: বাংলা হরফ).

Arial

Arial   **Arial Bold**

Arial Bold Italic   *Arial Italic*

Arial Black

Arial was designed in 1982 by a team, led by Robin Nicholas and Patricia Saunders, for Monotype Typography.

Arial is a contemporary sans serif design with humanist characteristics. Although it's extremely versatile, some people find Arial almost bland, which it's not.

Arial has the same metrics as Helvetica, with which it is often confused, although there plenty of differences in the design. This means that it's not a good idea to mix Arial and Helvetica next to one another in the same document.

The version included with Windows 8 features Arabic and Hebrew characters as well as Western, Central European, Turkish, Baltic, Cyrillic and Greek characters.

◻ Arial is one of the Microsoft ***Core fonts for the Web***.

abcdefghijklmnopqrstuvwxyz
abcdefghijklmnopqrstuvwxyz

Arial (top) compared to Helvetica (below): the spacing is the same, but the the most obvious differences are the tail of the 'a', the ascender on the 't', the crossbar on the 'f' and the thickness of the bowl where it joins the stem.

Calibri

Calibri   **Calibri Bold**

Calibri Bold Italic   *Calibri Italic*

Calibri Light   *Calibri Light Italic*

Calibri was designed by Lucas de Groot for Microsoft to serve as an example of what can be done by taking advantage of their ClearType rendering technology to to improve its readability on-screen.

Calibri includes WGL4 (Western, Central European, Turkish, Baltic, Cyrillic and Greek) characters.

Its OpenType features include small caps, subscripts and superscripts, and extra ligatures.

Cambria

Cambria   **Cambria Bold**

Cambria Bold Italic *Cambria Italic*

Cambria is a transitional serif font with very even spacing and proportions. Designed by Dutch typographer Jelle Bosma in 2004, with Steve Matteson and Robin Nicholas, this font family shows what can be done by using Microsoft's ClearType rendering.

Cambria includes WGL4 (Western, Central European, Turkish, Baltic, Cyrillic and Greek) characters, and its OpenType features include small caps, subscripts and superscripts, and extra ligatures.

BCÉGJQRSUßö 1428 $£
BCÉGJQRSUßö 1428 £$

Arial (top) compared to Helvetica (below): the upper case 'G' and 'Q' are the most obviously different but there are variations in the numerals and accented characters too.

Cambria Math

Cambria Math

Cambria Math is a variant of Cambria for use in mathematical, scientific and technical texts. It has all sorts of symbols, arrows and operators.

Candara

Candara   **Candara Bold**

Candara Bold Italic *Candara Italic*

Candara is a humanist sans-serif typeface which was designed to show what can be done by taking advantage of Microsoft's ClearType rendering technology to to improve its readability on-screen.

It includes WGL4 (Western, Central European, Turkish, Baltic, Cyrillic and Greek) characters.

Its OpenType features include automatic ligature sets, numerals (tabular, proportional, oldstyle and lining), numerator, denominator, scientific inferior subscripts, and small caps.

Comic Sans

Comic Sans MS   **Comic Sans MS Bold**

Comic Sans MS Bold Italic *Comic Sans MS Italic*

Comic Sans is a sans-serif casual script typeface, designed by Vincent Connare and first released by Microsoft in 1994. It's classified as a casual, non-connecting script, designed to imitate vintage comic book lettering, for use in informal documents.

It includes WGL4 (Western, Central European, Turkish, Baltic, Cyrillic and Greek) characters.

Its OpenType features include small caps, swashes, and extra ligatures.

- Comic Sans is one of the Microsoft ***Core fonts for the Web***.

28

Consolas

Consolas   **Consolas Bold**

Consolas Bold Italic   *Consolas Italic*

Consolas is a monospaced (non-proportional) typeface, designed by Luc(as) de Groot. It has a slash through the zero character.

This font family shows what can be done by taking advantage of Microsoft's ClearType rendering technology to to improve its readability on-screen.

Consolas's proportions, closer to normal text, make it more reader-friendly than, say, Courier New. It's the default monospaced font in Windows Vista, 7, 8 and 8.1 as well as the Office Suite.

Consolas is multilingual through the use of WGL4 (Western, Central European, Turkish, Baltic, Cyrillic and Greek) characters.

Its OpenType features include stylistic alternates, localized forms, uppercase-sensitive forms, old-style figures, lining figures, arbitrary fractions, superscript, subscript.

Constantia

Constantia   **Constantia Bold**

Constantia Bold Italic   *Constantia Italic*

Constantia, designed by John Hudson, is a serif typeface. It was first released as part of the Microsoft ClearType Font Collection, a set of fonts developed to take advantage of ClearType technology to improve on screen reading. However, it's equally suitable for use in books and other items where a serious look is needed.

It includes WGL4 (Western, Central European, Turkish, Baltic, Cyrillic and Greek) characters.

Its OpenType features include small caps, subscripts and superscripts, old-style figures, fractions, and extra ligatures.

Corbel

Corbel   **Corbel Bold**

Corbel Bold Italic   *Corbel Italic*

Corbel is a sans-serif typeface designed by Jeremy Tankard for Microsoft and released in 2005.

This font family makes use of ClearType rendering to improve its readability on-screen. It includes WGL4 (Western, Central European, Turkish, Baltic, Cyrillic and Greek) characters.

Its OpenType features include small caps, subscripts and superscripts, and extra ligatures.

Courier New

Courier New   **Courier New Bold**

Courier New Bold Italic *Courier New Italic*

The archetypical monospaced slab serif design, used to imitate typewriter output for reports, tabular work and technical documentation, Courier New originated as Adrian Frutiger's re-drawn version of IBM's Courier typewriter face for their Selectric range of golfball typewriters.

It supports Latin, Greek, Cyrillic, Arabic and Hebrew scripts as well as line drawing and other characters.

- Courier New is one of the Microsoft *Core fonts for the Web*.

Franklin Gothic

Franklin Gothic Medium   *Franklin Gothic Medium Italic*

Franklin Gothic is an extra-bold sans-serif type which dates back to by Morris Fuller Benton (1872–1948) in 1902.

It has WGL4 (Western, Central European, Cyrillic, Greek, Turkish, Baltic and line drawing) characters.

Gabriola

Gabriola

Gabriola is a display typeface designed by John Hudson and named after Gabriola Island, British Columbia, Canada.

Gabriola makes use of ClearType rendering for improve on-screen readability.

It includes WGL4 (Western, Central European, Turkish, Baltic, Cyrillic and Greek) characters. Its OpenType features include small caps, swashes, and extra ligatures.

- It only has *one weight* and *no italic*.

Georgia

Georgia   **Georgia Bold**

Georgia Bold Italic   *Georgia Italic*

Georgia is a transitional serif typeface designed in 1993 by Matthew Carter and hinted by Tom Rickner for Microsoft.

- Georgia is one of the Microsoft ***Core fonts for the Web***.

Impact

Impact

Impact is a realist sans-serif typeface which was designed in 1965 by Geoffrey Lee and originally released by the Stephenson Blake foundry. It has very thick strokes, minimal letterspacing and interior spaces. It's meant for headlines, not body text applications.

- Impact is one of the Microsoft ***Core fonts for the Web***.

It has WGL4 (Western, Central European, Cyrillic, Greek, Turkish, Baltic and line drawing) characters.

- It only has *one weight* and *no italic*.

Lucida Console

Lucida Console

Lucida Console is a monospaced font (actually a variant of Lucida Sans Typewriter with smaller line spacing) with WGL4 (Western, Central European, Cyrillic, Greek, Turkish, Baltic and line drawing) characters.

- ▫ It only has *one weight* and *no italic*.

Lucida Sans Unicode

Lucida Sans Unicode

Lucida Sans Unicode is designed to support the most commonly used characters defined in version 1.0 of the Unicode standard. It is a sans-serif variant of the Lucida font family and supports Latin, Greek, Cyrillic and Hebrew scripts, as well as all the letters used in the International Phonetic Alphabet.

- ▫ Lucida Sans Unicode only has *one weight* and *no italic*.

MS Sans Serif

Microsoft Sans Serif

Microsoft Sans Serif is a TrueType font that was designed as a direct replacement for the old MS Sans Serif bitmap system font.

- ▫ MS Sans Serif only has *one weight* and *no italic*.

Palatino Linotype

Palatino Linotype **Palatino Linotype Bold**

Palatino Linotype Bold Italic *Palatino Linotype Italic*

Palatino Linotype is an old style serif typeface. It's the 1999 revision of the original Palatino designed by Hermann Zapf and released in 1948 by Linotype. The revised version includes extended Latin, Greek, and Cyrillic character sets.

Segoe UI

Segoe UI	**Segoe UI Bold**
Segoe UI Bold Italic	*Segoe UI Italic*
Segoe UI Light	*Segoe UI Light Italic*
Segoe UI Semibold	***Segoe UI Semibold Italic***
Segoe UI Semilight	*Segoe UI Semilight Italic*

Segoe UI, its Light, Semibold and Semilight versions are part of the Segoe family used for the user interface by Microsoft software products as well as for some online user assistance material. Its use is intended to improve the consistency in how users see all text across all languages.

Segoe UI has a proper cursive italic, unlike the oblique used in Frutiger and Helvetica.

Segoe UI Symbol

Segoe UI Symbol ⇐ ⑥ ⚠

Segoe UI Symbol is a font that includes symbols such as chess pieces, playing cards and dice symbols, box-drawing characters, block elements, technical symbols, mathematical operators, arrows, control pictures, OCR, Braille patterns, Ogham and Runic text.

It is a Unicode-encoded font and the symbols are assigned to Unicode code points. The monospaced Segoe UI variant, and OCR characters are accessed By using OpenType stylistic sets.

Segoe Print

Segoe Print   **Segoe Print Bold**

Segoe Print is a font family based on the handwriting of Monotype Imaging employee Brian Allen, developed by Carl Crossgrove, James Grieshaber and Karl Leuthold.

- Segoe Print has normal and bold weights but no italics.

It has Western, Central European, Cyrillic, Greek, Turkish, Baltic and some line drawing/symbol characters.

Segoe Script

Segoe Script   Segoe Script Bold

Segoe Script is a font family designed by Carl Crossgrove, based on Brian Allen's handwriting, It mimics cursive handwriting and by using stylistic alternate OpenType feature, the unlinked letters become accessible.

- Segoe Script has normal and bold weights but no italics.

It has Western, Central European, Cyrillic, Greek, Turkish, Baltic and some line drawing/symbol characters.

Tahoma

Tahoma   **Tahoma Bold**

Tahoma is a humanist sans-serif typeface designed by Matthew Carter for Microsoft in 1994.

- Tahoma is one of the Microsoft *Core fonts for the Web*.
- Tahoma has normal and bold weights but *no italics*.

It supports Latin, Greek, Cyrillic and Hebrew scripts, as well as all the letters used in the International Phonetic Alphabet.

Times New Roman

Times New Roman   **Times New Roman Bold**

Times New Roman Bold Italic   *Times New Roman Italic*

Times New Roman is a serif typeface commissioned by *The Times* newspaper in 1931. Microsoft's version of Times New Roman licensed from Monotype matches the widths from the Adobe/Linotype version . It has the lighter capitals that were originally developed for printing in German.

The version included with Windows 8 features Arabic and Hebrew as well as Western, Central European, Turkish, Baltic, Cyrillic and Greek characters.

- Times New Roman is one of the Microsoft *Core fonts for the Web*.

Trebuchet MS

Trebuchet MS   **Trebuchet MS Bold**

Trebuchet MS Bold Italic   *Trebuchet MS Italic*

Trebuchet MS is a humanist sans-serif typeface designed by Vincent Connare for Microsoft in 1996. It is named after the trebuchet, a medieval siege engine.

- Trebuchet MS is one of the Microsoft ***Core fonts for the Web***.

Verdana

Verdana   **Verdana Bold**

Verdana Bold Italic*Verdana Italic*

Verdana is a humanist sans-serif typeface designed by Matthew Carter for Microsoft Corporation.

Verdana was designed to be readable at small sizes on a computer screen.

- Verdana is one of the Microsoft ***Core fonts for the Web***.

Symbol

Symbol   ABX 123 αβχ +?≅

Symbol is one of the four standard fonts available on all PostScript-based printers, including Apple's original LaserWriter from 1985. Windows has included Symbol as a core font since Windows 3.1x.

Its main purpose is for typesetting mathematical expressions. It contains a complete unaccented Greek alphabet (upper and lower case) and a selection of commonly used mathematical symbols.

Webdings

Webdings ◀ ◀◀ 🏕✔ ♥ 🎁 ✖ 🏔🌍⬤

Vincent Connare and his team developed Webdings in 1997. To start with, Webdings was part of Internet Explorer 4.0, but it's now one of Microsoft's *Core fonts for the Web*, and is included in all versions of Microsoft Windows.

Webdings has several families of similar symbols, such as weather icons, vehicles, globes and icons for use on signs.

- ᗡ The characters in this font are not have Unicode equivalents.

Wingdings

Wingdings 📑📇 ♦♋♎♏□ ☄✗✔■

Wingdings is a TrueType dingbat font designed by Charles Bigelow and Kris Holmes for Microsoft; it's been included with Windows since version 3.1.

Wingdings contains many widely recognised shapes and world symbols, such as the Star of David, Christian Cross, Buddhist yin-yang and the symbols of the zodiac.

- ᗡ The characters in this font do not correspond with a standard Unicode ranges, but many of its symbols are available in Unicode.

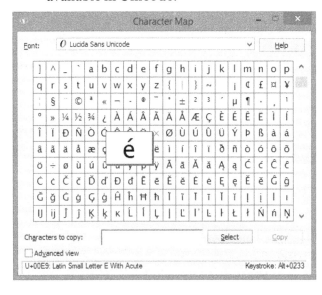

Windows Character Map displaying characters from Lucida Sans Unicode.

Points and picas

The **point** (usually abbreviated as *pt*) is the standard unit for measuring font size and leading and other minute items on a printed page.

There are 72 points to the inch, which makes one point approximately 0.0139 inch (or 0.3528 mm). Twelve points make up one **pica**, and six picas make one inch.

- This standardised point is very slightly different to the historical typographic point. It's usually known as a *DTP point* or (because of its use by Adobe in their PostScript® page description language) a *PostScript point*.

- The DTP point has almost entirely replaced earlier versions in day to day use.

Most novels and non-fiction books will use a fairly small type size for almost all of the text. 8.5 or 9.0 point text is quite typical.

The smaller the text, obviously, the more words can fit on one line. However, this makes it more difficult to follow when reading, as you might get lost when you reach the end of a line and not move on correctly to the next one. This is why newspapers and magazines tend to use multi-column layouts.

Eight or nine words per line or roughly 70-80 characters is about right for the small print area in a standard paperback novel but the lines in a newspaper with five or six columns might have only four or five words.

- On most desktop printers, text sized below 4.0 points will not be really legible. This applies particularly to ink jet printers if using 'ordinary' copy paper, because of ink being absorbed by the fibres in the paper.

One of the great things about desktop publishing is that it's so easy to make and preview changes. If you don't like the effect, simply change it back.

Paragraph Alignment

The way text is aligned affects its readability. Mostly, you will find that body text is either *left aligned* or *justified*. Headings are often centred.

Left aligned

The text in the paragraph below is aligned to the left ('flush left' or 'ragged right').

> Just over three years later Strousberg owned and operated iron foundries, coal mines, steelworks and rolling mills, engineering factories and plants for making rails, wagons and locomotives: a complete, vertically integrated industrial chain, from raw material to finished product.

Right aligned

The text in the paragraph below is aligned to the right ('flush right' or 'ragged left')

> Just over three years later Strousberg owned and operated iron foundries, coal mines, steelworks and rolling mills, engineering factories and plants for making rails, wagons and locomotives: a complete, vertically integrated industrial chain, from raw material to finished product.

Centred

The text in the paragraph below is aligned to the centre.

> Just over three years later Strousberg owned and operated iron foundries, coal mines, steelworks and rolling mills, engineering factories and plants for making rails, wagons and locomotives: a complete, vertically integrated industrial chain, from raw material to finished product.

Justified

The text in the paragraph below is justified, pushed out to align to both the right and left by adjusting the space between words.

> Just over three years later Strousberg owned and operated iron foundries, coal mines, steelworks and rolling mills, engineering factories and plants for making rails, wagons and locomotives: a complete, vertically integrated industrial chain, from raw material to finished product.

Justified text which isn't hyphenated tends to show visually unappealing 'rivers of white'.

On the the third line, the space between the word *steelworks* and the word *and* is overly large compared to the space between the word *over* and the word *three* on the first line.

Force justified

Force justified text looks almost the same as justified text, but if there are only a few words on the last line then they will be forced to the frame margins, with the space shared so that each gap on the line is the same size. If there is only one word on the last line of a force justified paragraph, then the effect is even worse.

> Just over three years later Strousberg owned and operated iron foundries, coal mines, steelworks and rolling mills, engineering factories and plants for making rails, wagons and locomotives: a complete, vertically integrated industrial chain, from the raw materials to finished product.

This is a very good reason *not* to use force justification.

To justify or not?

One rule of thumb on whether your line length is long enough to work if justified is that the *line length in picas* should be roughly *twice the point size of the type*.

So, if your type size is 12 points, the line length should be about 24 picas (4 inches or 10.16cm— 6 picas per inch).

You can work out the line length needed for effective justification for a particular type size easily.

- ◦ For example, for 9 point text, you'd really want a line length of at least 18 picas, that's 3 inches or 7.6cm.

Turn this around and you can work out the type size needed for effective justification for a particular line length.

- ◦ For example, for 2.5 inch line (15 picas), you'd want text no bigger than 7.5 points.

This is more of an issue for multi-column layouts like newspapers.

Research on readability has shown that inconsistent gaps between words are disruptive, and inhibit the flow of reading.

Usually, it's better to align type on the left and leave the right ragged.

Hyphenation

Hyphenation breaks words into two or more sections so that they fit better into the available space. Most DTP software hyphenates text automatically if its auto hyphenation option is enabled.

You need to be especially careful with non-English words if auto-hyphenation is on, because hyphenation rules are different in other languages. In German, if a hyphen falls between a **c** and a **k**, as in *drucken* (to print) the word becomes *druk-ken*.

Most DTP software will let you select a single word and mark it as being in a particular language to make that language's hyphenation rules apply to that word only.

Justified text which isn't hyphenated tends to show visually unappealing 'rivers of white'.

On the the third line, the space between the word *and* and the word *steelworks* is overly large compared to the space between the word *over* and the word *three* on the first line.

> Just over three years later Strousberg owned and operated iron foundries, coal mines, steelworks and rolling mills, engineering factories and plants for making rails, wagons and locomotives: a complete, vertically integrated industrial chain, from raw material to finished product.

With hyphenation, the first four letters of the word *steelworks* slide from the third to the second line and the first four letters of the word *locomotives* slide from the fifth to the fourth line.

> Just over three years later Strousberg owned and operated iron foundries, coal mines, steelworks and rolling mills, engineering factories and plants for making rails, wagons and locomotives: a complete, vertically integrated industrial chain, from raw material to finished product.

Leading, or linespace

The main rule is to keep the linespacing (the space between the lines of type) within a paragraph consistent.

The term leading dates back to typesetting with movable metal type, also known as letterpress printing. Each character was cast separately onto a tiny piece of metal (an alloy, mostly lead, but also antimony and tin). The characters were lined up in rows (composed), with small strips of blank metal (the leading) stuck between the rows to separate them.

Hot metal type was cast a whole line at a time using Linotype or similar machines,which saved arranging the lines one letter at a time, used the same principle. A strip of blank lead was inserted to separate the lines (the leading).

Type was–and is–measured in points, 72 points per inch. Logically, so's the leading. For example, if the type was 10 points high and the small strip of lead inserted between the lines was 2 points high the leading would be 12 point (size in points of the spacing strip plus the point size of the type) .

- Leading is usually expressed as a an absolute value, measured in point. For the example mentioned above, that is 10 point type on 12 point leading, it would be expressed as **10/12**.
- Leading can also be expressed as a percentage of the text point size. For 10/12, it would be 120%.
- Word processing software often uses simple terms like single line spacing. It's a little vague, but is usually about 125% of the text point size.

Adjusting line spacing makes text more or less difficult to read.

12/14 (12 point text on 14 point leading):

> Just over three years later he owned and oper-
> ated iron foundries, coal mines, steelworks and
> rolling mills, engineering factories and plants
> for making rails, wagons and locomotives: a
> complete, vertically integrated industrial chain,
> from raw material to finished product.

12/13 (12 point text on 13 point leading)::

> Just over three years later he owned and oper-
> ated iron foundries, coal mines, steelworks and
> rolling mills, engineering factories and plants
> for making rails, wagons and locomotives: a
> complete, vertically integrated industrial chain,
> from raw material to finished product.

12/12 (12 point text on 12 point leading):

> Just over three years later he owned and oper-
> ated iron foundries, coal mines, steelworks and
> rolling mills, engineering factories and plants
> for making rails, wagons and locomotives: a
> complete, vertically integrated industrial chain,
> from raw material to finished product.

As you can see, the reduction has a slight but noticeable effect.

Reducing the leading to less than the point size of the type with normal size text is generally *not a good idea.*

12/11 (12 point text on 11 point leading):

> Just over three years later he owned and oper-
> ated iron foundries, coal mines, steelworks and
> rolling mills, engineering factories and plants
> for making rails, wagons and locomotives: a
> complete, vertically integrated industrial chain,
> from raw material to finished product.

12/9 (12 point text on 9 point leading)

> Just over three years later he owned and oper-
> ated iron foundries, coal mines, steelworks and
> rolling mills, engineering factories and plants
> for making rails, wagons and locomotives: a
> complete, vertically integrated industrial chain,
> from raw material to finished product.

As you can see the descenders and ascenders clash and the density makes it hard to read the text. At 12/11 it's just about acceptable, but at 12/9 it's not.

Leading with all caps

Because capital letters have no descenders, there is an awkward-looking gap between lines of all capital letters (just about the only time you'd be using all caps is for headlines).

To fix this, you need to tighten up (that is, reduce) the leading. Firstly, work out what the auto leading is (120% or so of the pointsize). Then set the leading to less than that.

For example, the auto leading for 36 point type would be about 43 points, as in the example below where the space looks larger than it needs to be:

LAST MINE TO CLOSE

Usually, with all caps it's possible to actually reduce the leading to *less* than the point size of the type, for example 36 point type and 34 point leading:

LAST MINE TO CLOSE

Paragraph spacing

One thing which often catches people out is that hitting the Return key does not work the same way it did on a typewriter. On a typewriter, you have to hit the Return key at the end of each line to return the paper carriage mechanism to the left and advance to the next line.

With word processing or DTP software, this is **not** necessary.

Just carry on typing and the words will continue to the next line automatically, and a *soft return* is placed after the last character before the break. This is known as word wrap. The space between the lines in a paragraph—the leading—will stay the same.

When you do need to hit the Return key however is to begin a new paragraph. Each time you hit Return to insert a paragraph break or *hard return*, an extra space is inserted *after* the last line of the 'old' paragraph and *before* the 'new' paragraph.

Space before and Space after are part of the paragraph formatting attributes and it's best to set them as part of a style.

Kerning & Tracking

Kerning

Kerning is the process of modifying the space between individual pairs of letters so as to improve the appearance of the printed text.

It is used because the shapes of some pairs of letters result in a visually unattractive amount of white space between them when they are next to each other.

It's particularly noticeable with pairs of capital letters where there is a bold upright next to a slope, more so with sans-serif typefaces.

TADCASTER
TADCASTER

The need for kerning is more obvious with larger type, especially in posters or headlines.

Tracking

Tracking is similar to kerning but it refers to adjusting the amount of space between a group of letters (rather than the amount of space between a pair of letters) to affect density in a line or block of text.

For example you can apply tracking to tighten up the space between all of the letters in one word:

TADCASTER

TADCASTER

Conversely, you can apply tracking to loosen up the space between all of the letters in one word:

Tadcaster

Tadcaster

This is a useful technique for creating emphasis in blackletter typefaces which don't have bold or italic versions.

Unicode

Unicode is the international standard used to represent, encode and handle text expressed in most of the world's writing systems.

The latest version of Unicode contains over 110,000 characters in 100 scripts. Developed in conjunction with the Universal Character Set standard, it is published in book form as *The Unicode Standard*. The book is awkwardly large and expensive and so it's far easier to use the web site at **www.unicode.org** which is also updated more often.

The standard consists of

- a set of code charts for visual reference
- an encoding methodology and set of standard character encodings;
- a set of reference data computer files; and
- a number of related items (character properties, rules for normalization, decomposition, collation, rendering, and bidirectional display order[1]).

It covers almost all of the world's languages.

The standard way to write a Unicode character reference is U+(XXXX) where XXXX is a four character reference code.

In most programs, to insert a Unicode character you type the four character reference immediately followed by ALT+X.

- U+0416 for example is the reference for Ж (the CYRILLIC CAPITAL ZHE) so you would enter 0416, hold down the ALT key and press X.

Obviously, this only works if the font contains the relevant character.

---

[1] For the correct display of text containing both right-to-left scripts, such as Arabic and Hebrew, and left-to-right scripts

Spaces

Spaces after punctuation

With a typewriter, it was usual to add two spaces after a full stop to emphasise that it marked the end of a sentence. Adding two spaces after punctuation is not necessary when using desktop publishing software, so try not to do it.

Spaces between words

As far as most people are concerned there is only one sort of space, the one generated by pressing the spacebar on the keyboard. This is not the case as far as desktop publishing and typography are concerned.

The space generated by pressing the spacebar is what's known as a variable space. It can be stretched or shrunk by your software, and this can affect the way lines break.

Special spaces

Special spaces, which are generated *not* by pressing the spacebar but by inserting a Unicode reference code, are proportional to the font's point size.

Nonbreaking sp.	U+00A0	first last	
Em space	U+2003	first last	point size of font
En space	U+2002	first last	½ font point size
Quarter em space	U+2005	first last	¼ font point size
Punctuation space	U+2008	first last	width of full stop
Figure space	U+2007	first last	width of digit
Thin space	U+2009	first last	width of 1/5 em
Hair space	U+200A	firstlast	*less* than thin space

Use of these special spaces can help prevent words from wrapping onto the next line.

Be careful if you do use any of the special spaces as they can mess up justification, hyphenation and line breaks.

Emphasis

If you want to draw attention to a few words in a line, then there are several ways to do so.

- Put the *words to emphasise into italic* [bear in mind that not all fonts have a true italic].
- Put the **words to emphasise into bold** or even ***bold-italic***.
- <u>Underline the words to emphasise.</u> (Not recommended, because the underline cuts through any characters with a descender.)
- **Reverse-out the words to emphasise**.
- Put the `words to emphasise into a contrasting typeface`.
- Put the words to emphasise into a different colour. But be careful as your nice colour design might be copied in black and white and the emphasis is then lost.

The crucial thing to remember is that, like any attention grabbing feature, these effects can distract from the overall story and are best when used sparingly.

Bold, italic and bold-italic

The bold version of a typeface will usually be similar to the normal version but heavier in appearance.

The italic version of a typeface will usually be radically different to the normal version with all of the characters redrawn and some changing shape entirely.

&£?@ Aefghikpvwz
&£?@ Aefghikpvwz

Common shape changes include:

- a round or 'one-storey' a [*a* instead of a];
- an e whose bowl is curved rather than pointed [*e* instead of e];
- an f with a tail [*f* instead of **f**];
- a k with a looped bowl instead of a straight diagonal spur [*k* not **k**];

- a k with a ball terminal;
- a p with an intersection at the stem (ascender);
- v and w with swashes and curved bottoms [*v* instead of **v**]; and
- a *z* with the stress on the horizontal strokes, not the diagonal vertical one.

These differences won't always be included. The *a* and *f* usually are, but the *k* often isn't.

According to the typeface, there might also be very pronounced changes in, for example, the ampersand.

Usually, if a word is set in italic then the space *afterwards* is italicised too, producing a slightly narrower space which is supposed to be visually more pleasing.

Another technique sometimes used with italics is to set them *slightly larger* than the surrounding text. However this needs to be done consistently, ideally using a character style.

The ***bold-italic*** version of a typeface will usually be similar to the italic version but heavier in appearance.

- Some typefaces are specifically designed without bold and italic variants. Your software might let you apply a synthesised bold or italic effect, but you should be wary of doing so. Apart from design considerations, there might be output problems with high-end print or PDF production.

Underlining

Underlining is also a legacy from the days of typewriter use, when it was the only method of emphasis available. Even so, it was a fiddly job. Thankfully being able to use *italics* or **bold** is a better alternative.

The main drawback of underlined text is that the underline <u>slices through</u> any characters with a descender, punctuation marks or accents which are below the baseline.

It's especially ugly when combined with headline size reversed out text, although that does not seem to put newspapers off using it.

Drop caps

Drop caps, short for *dropped capitals*, are yet another way of showing the importance of a paragraph, especially at the start of an article or chapter.

You should be very careful as some letters like L leave an ugly gap before the text proper.

Just over three years later he owned and operated iron foundries, coal mines, steelworks and rolling mills, engineering factories and plants for making rails, wagons and locomotives: a complete, vertically integrated industrial chain, from raw material to finished product.

Quotation Marks

'Proper' typographic single quotation marks (' and ') and double quotation marks (" and ") [also called curly quotes] are usually used in DTP documents.

Using a pair of apostrophes (' and ') and ordinary quotation marks (" and ") otherwise known as straight quotes is really a relic from typewriters.

- In US usage, a LEFT DOUBLE QUOTATION MARK goes before the quotation and a RIGHT DOUBLE QUOTATION MARK follows it. For speech-in-speech, a LEFT SINGLE QUOTATION MARK goes before the quotation and a RIGHT SINGLE QUOTATION MARK follows it.

- In UK usage, a LEFT SINGLE QUOTATION MARK goes before the quotation and a RIGHT SINGLE QUOTATION MARK follows it. For speech-in-speech, a LEFT DOUBLE QUOTATION MARK goes before the quotation and a RIGHT DOUBLE QUOTATION MARK follows it.

Some programs have an option which will change straight quotes to typographic quotes automatically as you type, but this only applies to text entered in the program. Straight quotes in text imported from a file will remain unchanged.

Quotation marks in other languages

Different typographic quotation marks are used in languages other than English.

French quotation marks

In French, double angle quotation marks are used.

- A left-pointing double angle quotation mark goes before the quotation and a RIGHT-POINTING DOUBLE ANGLE QUOTATION MARK follows it. The same goes for speech-in-speech.

- Swiss French uses a LEFT-POINTING SINGLE ANGLE QUOTATION MARK in front of, and a RIGHT-POINTING

SINGLE ANGLE QUOTATION MARK following, speech-in-speech.

> « Je ne suis pas d'accord avec ce que vous dites, mais je défendrai jusqu'à la mort votre droit de le dire ».

Tthere's a small space between the speech mark and the words. (Strictly speaking, this should be a quarter-em space in typography, but most of the time people use an ordinary spacebar space because non-Unicode fonts don't have a quarter-em space and there's no way to enter a non-breaking space with a single keystroke).

German quotation marks

In German the opening quotation mark is placed on the baseline, like this „ and the closing quotation mark is the same as the English opening quotation mark ".

▫ In Germany and Austria, a DOUBLE LOW-9 QUOTATION MARK goes before the quotation and a LEFT DOUBLE QUOTATION MARK follows it. For speech-in-speech, a SINGLE LOW-9 QUOTATION MARK goes before the quotation and a LEFT SINGLE QUOTATION MARK follows it.

> „Kind," sagte der Vater mitleidig und mit auffallendem Verständnis, „was sollen wir aber tun?"

In printed media like books, newspapers or magazines, you can often find angle quotation marks either single or double used instead.

> »Kind,« sagte der Vater mitleidig und mit auffallendem Verständnis, »was sollen wir aber tun?«

Note that in Swiss German, French-style angle quotation marks (pointing the other way) may be used.

Spanish quotation marks

Spanish uses angle quotation marks like French but without a space between the speech mark and the words.

- ◻ A LEFT-POINTING DOUBLE ANGLE QUOTATION MARK goes before the quotation and a RIGHT-POINTING DOUBLE ANGLE QUOTATION MARK follows it.

  > «Los centros territoriales de Televisión Española y Radio Nacional te acercan a la actualidad de tu comunidad autónopma. Información regional y local, con la calidad de RTVE.».

- ◻ Spanish uses a LEFT DOUBLE QUOTATION MARK before the quotation and a RIGHT DOUBLE QUOTATION MARK after the quotation to show speech-in-speech.

Note that there's no space between the speech mark and the words.

Dutch quotation marks

Modern-day Dutch uses typographic single quotation marks (' and ') and double quotation marks (" and ") as in UK English.

> 'Onze kerntaken zijn, kwaliteitsbewaking informatievoorziening en informeren ondernemers en TIP's.'

Some newspapers still use the old style with a SINGLE LOW-9 QUOTATION MARK before the quote and a RIGHT SINGLE QUOTATION MARK after it.

> ‚Onze kerntaken zijn, kwaliteitsbewaking informatievoorziening en informeren ondernemers en TIP's.'

Finnish quotation marks

Finnish normally uses a pair of RIGHT DOUBLE QUOTATION MARKS, one at either end of the quotation.

> ”Mutta yksi pykälä on meillä kohta suoritettavana. Tämä on laita: Jos talonpitoomme toivomme järjestystä ja pysyväisyyttä, niin yksi olkoon esimies ja isäntä.”

Alternatively a pair of RIGHT-POINTING DOUBLE ANGLE QUOTATION MARKS are sometimes used.

> » Me tiedämme, että tämä oikeus ja velvollisuus on Juhanin sekä hänen esikoisuutensa että äitimme määräyksen kautta. »

◦ Finnish uses a pair of RIGHT SINGLE QUOTATION MARKS, one at either end of the quote to mark speech-in-speech.

Italian quotation marks

Italian uses angle quotation marks like French but without a space between the speech mark and the words.

◦ A LEFT-POINTING DOUBLE ANGLE QUOTATION MARK goes before the quotation and a RIGHT-POINTING DOUBLE ANGLE QUOTATION MARK follows it.

> « L'incremento delle accise si è rivelato finora il metodo più efficace per spingere i consumatori ad acquistare veicoli più "parsimoniosi" e meno inquinanti. ».

◦ Italian uses a LEFT DOUBLE QUOTATION MARK before the quotation and a RIGHT DOUBLE QUOTATION MARK after it to show speech-in-speech.

◦ Swiss Italian uses a LEFT-POINTING SINGLE ANGLE QUOTATION MARK before and a RIGHT-POINTING SINGLE ANGLE QUOTATION MARK following, speech-in-speech.

Quotation marks in Unicode

Glyph	Code	Unicode name
"	U+0022	quotation mark
'	U+0027	apostrophe
«	U+00AB	left-pointing double angle quotation mark
»	U+00BB	right-pointing double angle quotation mark
'	U+2018	left single quotation mark
'	U+2019	right single quotation mark
‚	U+201A	single low-9 quotation mark
‛	U+201B	single high-reversed-9 quotation mark
"	U+201C	left double quotation mark
"	U+201D	right double quotation mark
„	U+201E	double low-9 quotation mark
‟	U+201F	double high-reversed-9 quotation mark
‹	U+2039	single left-pointing angle quotation mark
›	U+203A	single right-pointing angle quotation mark

Accents

Accents (or *diacritics*) are markings placed above, below or through characters to alter their pronunciation or meaning.

English doesn't use accented characters, except in words borrowed from other languages, and so UK keyboards don't have accented characters on them.

For the accents needed in Western languages, enter the accented character by holding down the ALT key and entering *<nnnn>* (a four-digit number) with the numeric keypad.

For the accents needed in other languages, you need to enter the Unicode reference. In most programs, to insert a Unicode character you type the four character reference immediately followed by ALT+X.

- 015E for example is the reference for Ş (Capital S with cedilla) so you would enter 015E and then hold down the ALT key and press X.

Obviously, this only works if the font contains the relevant character.

The dot on the lowercase i was originally used to make it distinct from the vertical strokes of adjacent letters. Later on, the j, which is closely related, used the dot (shaped like a long flourish in medieval times, shrinking to the familiar round dot).

Em and en dashes

You can use em and en dashes ('—' and '–') instead of a simple hyphen ('-') when a pair of dashes is used instead of brackets.

- An em-dash is usually generated by holding down the ALT key and typing 0151 on the numeric keypad.
- An en-dash is half the width of an em-dash and is usually generated by holding down the ALT key and typing 0150 on the numeric keypad.

Some programs allow em and en dashes to be inserted from a menu.

Styles

Styles are collections of formatting attributes, grouped so that they can be applied together. By using the style management feature in your DTP software, you can apply changes to the whole document at once. Styles are the best way to keep text formatting consistent throughout a publication (or series of publications) to build up a house style. Most DTP software has two types of text style, *paragraph styles* and *character styles*.

Paragraph styles

A paragraph style contains all of the formatting information needed for a paragraph. This includes all character formatting attributes, and the paragraph formatting attributes.

Character styles

A character style on the other hand only contains character formatting attributes (such as the font name, point size, style and so on) and is applied to selected characters only.

Paragraph formatting attributes

Paragraph formatting attributes include:

- Alignment, and spacing (including leading, indents, space before and space after);
- Hyphenation options;
- Justification options (including word and letter spacing);
- bullets and numbering options;
- Breaks (e.g. widow and orphan control);
- Line above/below paragraph.

Character formatting attributes

Character formatting attributes include:

- Font options (including typeface name, size, style, fill and background colour);
- Spacing options (including optical justification);
- OpenType options;
- Language.

OpenType

What is OpenType?

OpenType® is a cross-platform standard for computer font files, developed jointly by Adobe and Microsoft. The same font file works on both Mac and Windows.

The OpenType format is a development of TrueType's SFNT format, but it can also make use of Adobe® PostScript® (Type 1) font data, as well as its own new typographic layout features.

On Windows computers, PostScript-derived OpenType files have the extension .OTF whereas TrueType-based OpenType fonts have a .TTF extension.

OpenType® fonts can support expanded character sets and layout features. A single font file can support several languages and include extra glyphs (the shapes which make up the drawn form of the character), grouped into sets of typographic features.

Used carefully, they make the text look better in print.

Common OpenType layout features

Ligatures

Ligatures use a single glyph to run two or three characters together. Perhaps the best-known standard ligature is 'fi' which combines 'f' and 'i', and means the dot of the 'i' does not clash with the top of the 'f'. As a reader, you often don't consciously notice that standard ligatures are being used, but discretionary ligatures like 'st' for 'st' are more obvious; they often look old fashioned or too ornate for ordinary text.

Stylistic sets and alternates

Stylistic sets and alternates can be ornate or flowing ('swash') versions of a glyph. They may also include things like a 'g' with and without a closed descender, or zero with and without a slash.

Small Caps

A Small Caps 'a' is the same shape as a capital 'A' but smaller. Obviously, this could be done by simple scaling a capital 'A' to a smaller point size, but that would make the stem widths too thin. Okay on screen, but it can look slightly wrong in print. Some fonts have a Small Caps 'a' that is actually redrawn and not just scaled.

Petite Caps

Petite Caps are like Small Caps but even smaller. A font might also provide special character forms for use in titles, that look better at large sizes.

Case sensitive forms

Case sensitive forms are variants of punctuation such as brackets, that are designed to align better with capitals. They generally sit a little higher in the line, as capital letters (except for Q) don't have descenders.

Superscripts and subscripts

Superscripts and subscripts are smaller raised or lowered versions of characters; the scaling issues are the same as for Small Caps. Some fonts also have *ordinals*, a form of superscript which can be used for the letters in 2nd, 3rd, 4th and so on or some chemical and mathematical notation.

Fractions

The digits before the stroke become smaller and raised, and the digits following the stroke become smaller and may be lowered. For example, 1/87 becomes $\frac{1}{87}$. A special narrow version of the stroke may be used.

Old style figures

Old style figures [1234567890] are digits with a bit more character than the usual lining figures [1234557890] . They vary in height, sit lower in the line are often used in body text.

Proportional figures

Proportional figures are variable width digits; for example, a '1' that is narrower than a '2' instead of the more usual tabular figures that are all the same width (so they line up in columns or tables).

Opticals

Opticals are optimised for use at specific point sizes. These vary for each particular typeface, but are usually in the ranges 6-8 point (caption), 9-13 point (regular), 14-24 point (subhead) and 25-72 point (display).

Character sets

OpenType fonts can (but do not have to) include multiple language character sets in one font.

- Adobe's OpenType fonts have the 'usual' Latin characters, and some 'international' characters, such as the "estimated" (℮) and litre (ℓ) symbols used on food packaging and the euro currency symbol (€).

- Adobe's OpenType Pro fonts and some of Microsoft's OpenType fonts have all of the accented characters needed for central and eastern European languages, such as Romanian, Lithuanian and Polish. Many of these fonts also contain Cyrillic and Greek characters and one or two even include Arabic and Hebrew (these are right-to-left scripts; not all software can use them properly).

Glyphs

One character may correspond to several glyphs. Lowercase "a", small cap "a" and an alternate swash lowercase "a" are all the same character, but they are three separate glyphs.

One glyph can represent multiple characters, like the **ffi** ligature, which represents the sequence of three characters: f, f and i.

Applying OpenType features to characters can alter the positioning, or substitute a different glyph. Applying the small capitals feature to the "a" changes the the usual lowercase "a" glyph for the small cap "A" glyph.

Software needs a dialog or tab to let you use the alternative glyphs in OpenType fonts. If you're using an application which doesn't support Unicode or advanced OpenType features you can still access the basic glyph sets (they're similar to the glyph sets in PostScript Type 1 fonts).

Colour?

We all know—or think we know—what a colour is.

Colour plays a very important role, both psychologically and aesthetically, in designing both for print and for the web.

Colour is represented on a computer monitor by mixing Red, Green, and Blue light (lighting up red, green or blue pixels), but it is represented in 4-colour process printing by mixing Cyan, Yellow, Magenta and Black inks on the paper.

Because of this, the colours which appear on screen will never quite match the colours which appear in printed output.

Colour design considerations

There are a large number of design considerations when designing some- thing which is going to be printed, or appear on the web, in colour.

Colour combinations

Certain colour combinations just do not work together.

- In general, if there is little contrast between the background and the text colour, then the text is hard to read, so it is best to stick to fairly plain colours with a high contrast between them for body text.

This seems not to apply to banks or mobile phone providers. Dark grey text on a light grey background might look cool on screen but it'll look awful if it's photocopied.

Some high contrast colours do not work either, for example, blue text on a red background, or red on bright green, and so on.

Partial red/green colour blindness is surprisingly common, although complete inability to distinguish colours is rare (in Britain you can't be a train driver if you're colour blind).

Culture clash

In different parts of the world, colours might mean different things. These are just a few examples.

- Red is for danger but is also the colour for good luck in the Chinese culture. Politically, it usually stands for socialism or communism.

- Yellow and black stripes are often used to draw attention to warning signs and notices.

- Green is usually taken to signify safety, for example in the mandatory emergency exit signs used in Europe.
As a flag colour, it often symbolises Islam (for example the field of the Saudi Arabian flag).
It is also the colour used internationally by "environment-friendly" organisations.

- Black is the colour of mourning in many countries, but in some cultures the colour of mourning is white.

Production method considerations

Most obviously, designs which work well in colour probably will not look good in black and white. This means the output method really must be considered at the design stage.

- If printing on a colour inkjet, fine lines might merge into each other due to the limitations of inkjet printing.

- Desktop colour printers have cyan, yellow, magenta and black cartridges (some have 'light' colours too) but they are fed an RGB signal from the computer, which is converted to CMYK by the printer's on-board firmware.

If the design is already in CMYK then it is converted *twice*: to RGB for sending to the printer and then back to CMYK in the printer.

CMYK designs look dull when viewed on screen.

RGB or CMYK?

A monitor displays a colour image by illuminating a combination of red, green and blue pixels (hence, RGB).

- Mix all three colours together to get white light.
- Turn all the elements off to get black.

- The range of colours it is possible to mix with a given process is referred to as a colour gamut. RGB has an almost infinite gamut.

On the other hand, CMYK printing creates colours by mixing inks and absorbing light.

- Mix the cyan, magenta and yellow inks and the result is a very dark brown, almost but not quite black. That's why the pure black (the K in CMYK) is added.
- No ink gives white (or the colour of the paper).

CMYK is a subtractive model, whereas RGB is an additive model.

The RGB gamut is much larger than the CMYK gamut.

CMYK is not better than RGB. It is however different.

Paper and page sizes

All publications are made up of **pages** and **spreads**.

- A **spread** is what the reader sees when he or she opens a book or folded publication and consists of a **pair of adjacent pages**.
- The **even-numbered page is on the left** and the **odd-numbered page is on the right**.

Books, magazines and newspapers all treat pages and spreads differently but they will use an underlying grid of some sort.

Before looking at how pages and spreads are laid out, it's a good idea to consider the issue of paper sizes. As far as desktop publishing goes, the vast majority of home and office printers use small sheets: A4 (or US Letter) which of course puts a huge constraint on page layout. Of course, DTP software will happily cope with bigger sizes.

Desktop printer paper sizes

Desktop output basically comes down to photocopying or printing multiple copies on the printer linked to the PC. The vast majority of desktop laser or inkjet printers are limited to A4/US Letter-sized output as a maximum. A3/Tabloid printers are less common.

Professional print paper sizes

- Sheet-fed offset and digital presses use large sheets which are cut down to the exact size after printing. If need be they're folded and collated as well.
- Web offset presses are fed from huge reels of paper, often metres wide and weighing over a tonne. They're mostly used for newspapers, magazines and books.

DIN and ISO paper sizes

ISO, the international standards body, has issued three almost globally used standards. ISO 216 defines the 'A' and 'B' series; ISO 217 and ISO 269 define related paper sizes[1]. They all have the same aspect ratio, 1:$\sqrt{2}$ which is 'magic' as if a sheet is folded or cut in two widthwise then both pieces have the same aspect ratio.

The idea's not new. In 1786 the German physicist Georg Christoph Lichtenberg noted the possible uses of paper sizes based on an aspect ratio of 1:$\sqrt{2}$. In 1798 in France, the revolutionary government defined several formats virtually identical to some modern ISO paper sizes[2], although it never became widely known and quickly fell out of use.

Fast forward to the early 1920s and Berlin mathematician Dr Walter Porstmann made Lichtenberg's idea into a proper system of different paper sizes. Porstmann's system was adopted by his employer, the *Deutsche Institut für Normung* (the German Institute for Standardisation) becoming DIN standard 476 in 1922. It quickly replaced many other paper formats. In everyday use in Germany and Austria the paper sizes are still often called *DIN A4, DIN A3* and so on .

Paper using the golden ratio scales well. Folded brochures of any size can be made by using sheets of the next larger size, for example A4 sheets folded to make A5 brochures. As another example, a 16 page A4 newsletter will print on an A1 sheet.

- The weight of each sheet is also easy to calculate as the basis weight is quoted in grams per square metre (g/m^2 or gsm).

- An A0 sheet has an area of 1 m^2 and so its weight in grams is the same as its basis weight in g/m^2. An A4

---

[1] ISO 216:1975, defines the A and B series of paper sizes

ISO 269:1985, defines the C series for envelopes

ISO 217:1995, defines the RA and SRA series of raw ("untrimmed") paper sizes

[2] Loi sur le timbre (no. 2136), (a law on the taxation of paper) defined several formats virtually identical to some modern ISO paper sizes: "Grand registre" (A2), "grand papier" (B3), "moyen papier" (A3), "petit papier" (B4), "demi feuille" (1B5), "effets de commerce" (1/2 B5).3

sheet of 80 g/m² paper weighs 5 g, as it is one 16th (four halvings) of an A0 page.

- If you're in charge of sending out a newsletter or mailshot, this lets you work out the weight (and the associated postage rate) easily, by counting the number of sheets used.

A series paper has an aspect ratio of 1:√2 (1:1.41), rounded to the nearest millimetre. A0 is defined so that it has an area of 1 square metre before rounding. Successive paper sizes in the series (A1, A2, A3, etc.) are defined by halving the preceding paper size, cutting parallel to its shorter side (the long side of A4 (297mm) is the same length as the short side of A3 and the short side of A4 (210mm) is the same length as the long side of A5).

A4 is 210 mm × 297 mm (8.3 in × 11.7 in). Letter size as used in North America (8.5 in × 11 in (220 mm × 280 mm)) is a bit wider and not as tall as A4.

B series paper makes use of the ratio 1:√2 in a similar manner to the A series The lengths of the B series have the ratio 1:√2. Folding one sheet in half gives the next in the series. The shorter side of B0 is exactly 1m.

C series formats are used mainly for envelopes. They're geometric means between the B series and A series formats with the same number (for example, C2 is the geometric mean between B2 and A2). It uses the same width to height ratio as the A and B series, so an A4 sheet will fit into a C4 envelope. If an A4 sheet is folded in half so that it is A5 in size, it will fit into a C5 envelope (which will be the same size as a C4 envelope folded in half). The lengths of ISO C series paper are about 9% larger than A series.

The standard allows some tolerance in cut sizes (±1.5 mm for dimensions up to 150 mm, ±2.0 mm for dimensions in the range 150 to 600 mm, and ±3.0 mm for dimensions above 600 mm). This makes the maximum possible size for an A4 sheet 212mm × 299mm.

American paper sizes and weights

When it comes to paper for desktop printers, US sizes are the standard in the United States, the Philippines and Chile.

- "Letter" is defined as 8½in × 11in
- "Legal" size paper is 8½in × 14in in the US
- "Legal" size paper is 8½in × 13in in the Philippines and Chile
- "Tabloid" is defined as 11in × 17in

In Canada, US sizes are the *de facto* standard. The government uses a mix of ISO and US paper sizes set out in its own document. *"Paper Sizes for Correspondence"* (CAN 2-9.60M) specifies P1 through P6 paper sizes, based on the US paper sizes rounded to the nearest 5 mm.

Mexico (in theory) uses the ISO standard, but US formats are still the everyday norm. *"Carta 216 mm × 279 mm"* (letter), *"Oficio 216 mm × 330 mm"* (Government-Legal) and *"Doble carta"* (ledger/tabloid) are pretty much universal. US paper sizes are also widely used in Colombia and Venezuela.

In North America basis weight is used for defining the weight of paper and card. Confusingly, basis weight is defined as the weight of a ream—500 sheets—of the uncut paper in pounds (lb).

- The *uncut paper size* refers to the size used during manufacturing before the paper is cut to size.
- Each type of uncut paper or card has a *different uncut sheet size*.

Bond Stock, Cover Stock and Index Stock are the normal types used to make office paper and card.

- One sheet of 20lb Bond Letter paper will be the exactly the same thickness as one sheet of 20lb Bond Legal as both are cut from 20lb Bond stock. Obviously the two sheets will weigh different amounts because of the difference in size.

- One sheet of 28lb Bond Letter size paper would ***not*** be the same as a sheet of 28lb Cover Letter size paper because *the uncut sizes for Bond and Cover are different.*
- 'Stock' is often left out when referring to the different types of paper in their finished cut sizes.

Office paper is usually 20lb or 24lb Bond, and suppliers often don't put Bond on the pack, just giving the basis weight of 20lb or 24lb (# is often used instead of lb when referring to basis weights), but Index and Cover are almost invariably used as this differentiates the other types from the 'usual' Bond.

- 60lb and 65lb Cover and 90lb and 110lb Index are types of light to medium card often used as file dividers.
- 80lb, 90lb and 100lb Cover are heavier weight card.

The grades of stock most often used for professional printing are:

- ***Book paper***, named after its primary use in book printing, and designed to be a strong lightweight paper which is suitable for double sided printing. Its uncut size is 25 × 38in.
- ***Offset paper*** which is used in offset litho printing and digital printing as the paper is resistant to tearing. Its uncut size is 25 × 38in.
- ***Text paper*** which is generally coloured and has more surface texture than Bond stock. Its uncut size is 25 × 38in.
- ***Tissue*** which is an ultra lightweight paper type, often coloured and used in packaging or art and craft work.
- ***Newsprint*** stock is thin and light. It measures 24 × 36in uncut size, much larger than the Bond uncut size of 17 × 22in or Cover uncut size of 20 × 26in.

30lb Newsprint is actually a lot thinner than 20lb Bond.

Glossary

Accent	A mark placed above, below or through a character to indicate that it is pronounced differently to the character without an accent.
Ascender	The part of a lower-case letter which extends above the x-height.
Baseline	The imaginary line upon which characters or words sit.
Baseline	The line upon which most letters sit and below which descenders extend.
Berliner	Newspaper size, 12.4in × 18½in 315mm × 470mm
Bitmap	Pattern of tiny dots which make up an image.
Blackletter	Solid looking typeface based on the letter forms used in early printing, such as *Excalibur SF* or *WeddingText BT*. Often used for titles or place cards but hard to read in large amounts or in small sizes.
Bleed	The term used to describe a colour or fill which runs right to the page edge.
Bold	Variant of a typeface which is heavier than normal.
Broadsheet	**Newspaper size,** 15in × 22¾in 749mm × 557mm
Cap-height	The height of a capital letter.
CMYK	Abbreviation for Cyan, Yellow, Magenta, Key.
Descender	The part of a letter which dangles below the base line, for example the tail of a lowercase *q*.
Dingbat	Description for typefaces where the characters are icons or shapes, such as Wingdings.
DTP	Abbreviation for desktop publishing
Em	Typographical measure equal to the point size of the current font. 1 em in a 16 point typeface is 16 points (that is 0.222 inches) but in 12 point type it is 0.166 inches.
Em-dash	A dash which is one em in length.
Em-space	A space equal to the point size of the current font.

En	Typographical unit, half of the width of an em, that is half of the height of the font (for example in 16 point type it is 8 points). Traditionally the width of a lowercase letter n.
En-dash	A dash which is one en in length.
En-space	An space one en in width.
Font	Strictly speaking, one weight and size of a typeface, but tends to be use interchangeably with typeface.
Fraktur	A stereotypically Germanic blackletter typeface.
Glyphs	The shapes which make up the drawn form of the character.
Hinting	Mathematical instructions used to adjust the display of an outline font so that it lines up with the pixels on a screen to give clear, legible text.
Italic	Variant of a typeface which slopes to the right and has different letter-forms to the normal version.
Kerning	The process of adjusting letter spacing in a proportional font. In a well-kerned font, the spaces between each pair of letters all have similar area.
Landscape	Page which is wider than it is tall.
Letterspacing	Also called tracking, this refers to the amount of space between a group of letters to affect density in a line or block of text.
Ligature	A single glyph used to replace consecutive characters which have common components. The glyph's form is dependent on context.
Lowercase	Small letters as opposed to capital letters.
Monospaced	Typeface where all of the characters occupy the same amount of space (for example `Courier New` or `Consolas`).
PANTONE®	Colour matching standard for printing, commercially developed by Pantone, Inc.
PDF	Abbreviation for *Portable Document Format*, cross-platform file format originally developed by Adobe and now the de facto DTP document exchange format.

Pica	Unit of measurement in typography. Six picas make one inch. Twelve points make one pica.
Point	Unit of measurement for type, in DTP generally $\frac{1}{72}$ of an inch.
Portrait	Page which is taller than it is wide.
Proportional	Typeface in which the characters are not all the same width.
RGB	Abbreviation for Red, Green, Blue.
Rivers of white	Visually unattractive gaps which appear to trickle down a page. More noticeable if justification is used without hyphenation.
Sans-serif	Typeface without any protruding 'wings' at the end of ascenders, descenders or crosspieces, such as Arial or Verdana.
Script	Typefaces which imitates formal copperplate script; often used for invitations. Examples include *Embassy BT* and *English 157 BT*.
Serif	Typeface which has protruding 'wings' at the end of ascenders, descenders or crosspieces, such as Georgia or Palatino Linotype.
Sheet-fed	Press which prints on large sheets of paper.
Signature	Sheet which has been printed but not folded.
Tabloid	Newspaper size, 11in × 17in 432mm × 279mm
Typeface	A 'family' of characters which are similar in appearance, such as Palatino Linotype which has normal, *italic*, **bold** and ***bold italic*** versions.
Unicode	International standard for referring to characters.
Upper-case	Capital letters: the term dates back to moveable type, when capital letters were kept in a separate case stored above small letters.
Variable space	The space between word or characters produced by using the spacebar.
Web-fed	Printing press fed with paper from a reel of paper.
widows and orphans	Words or short lines at the beginning or end of a paragraph, which are left dangling at the top or bottom of a column, separated from the rest of the paragraph.

Comparison of A,B and C series

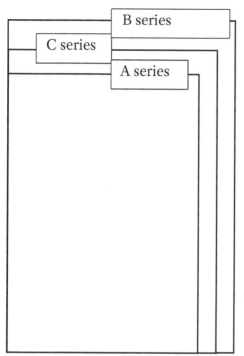

The diagram on the left shows how the ISO A, B and C sizes relate to one another.

The C series is usually used for envelopes for example you'd use a C5 envelope for A4 folded once to make A5.

Passports almost always use B7 size, which is the size specified by the International Civil Aviation Organisation.

	A series	B series	C series
0	840×1188mm	1000 × 1414mm	917 × 1297mm
1	594 × 840mm	707 × 1000mm	648 × 917mm
2	420 × 594mm	500 × 707mm	548 × 648mm
3	297 × 420mm	353 × 500mm	324 × 548mm
4	210 × 297mm	250 × 353mm	229 × 324mm
5	148 × 210mm	176 × 250mm	162 × 229mm
6	105 × 148mm	125 × 176mm	114 × 162mm
7	74 × 105mm	88 × 125mm	81 × 114mm
8	52 × 74mm	62 × 88mm	57 × 81mm
9	37 × 52mm	44 × 62mm	40 × 57mm
10	26 × 37mm	31 × 44mm	28 × 40mm

www.ingramcontent.com/pod-product-compliance
Lightning Source LLC
Chambersburg PA
CBHW051211050326
40689CB00008B/1273